Give Ease a Chance

Angelika Ruppert

Give Ease a Chance

- Tools for an Easy, Conscious Living -

Bibliographic information of the German National Library:

The German National Library lists this publication in the German National Bibliography; detailed bibliographic data are available on the Internet at http://dnb.dnb.de.

Manufactured & published by:
BoD - Books on Demand, Norderstedt, Germany
ISBN: 978-3-84826-466-7

Angelika Ruppert

Give Ease a Chance

- Tools for an Easy, Conscious Living -

Introduction

For years now I've been regularly applying all the different methods you will find in this book. The experiences and insights I've gained through them have helped me a lot on my path.

They've brought a new kind of easiness into my life. I now follow my impulses and embark on projects I would have described only a few years ago as *impossible to realize*.

Again and again new potentials show up in my life and I joyfully bring them into reality. One of these potentials was to write a book, this book.

Enjoy reading and experiencing it.

8

Give Ease a Chance

*In my Opinion
the secret of life is
to take things very, very easy.*
Oscar Wilde

Life can be so easy!

We often just don't have the necessary tools to move out of unwanted, difficult or uncomfortable situations. Far too often we believe we have no choice, we feel weak, powerless and stuck in a place where we actually don't want to be.

Why are we behaving in this way?

There are certainly many different reasons for this. At school, for example, we learn a lot 'for life', but we are not taught how to deal with situations when things turn out differently than we would have wanted them to be or when we get caught up in mind chatter.

Our parents didn't have the knowledge either to teach us, because they also had never learned it.

And that's why as grown-ups we go through difficult ordeals, therapies and processing our issues – again and again processing the issues – until eventually we realize, that we are constantly circling around the same subjects and that every answer just brings up new questions … what a vicious circle!

Our safety, too, seems to be outrageously important for us. That's why most of the time we avoid making changes so as not to jeopardize it. "It could all get *even* worse", we tell ourselves when we are confronted with situations we don't like and … it does get worse, precisely *because* we don't make a change.

Being stuck, not moving forward when actually every fiber within us cries for a change, brings us to the point where we experience more and more external impulses to move us forward.

If we continue to ignore these impulses, incidents will occur, which we then interpret as being struck by fate. Eventually we are *forced* to make a change, often from a place of deep suffering.

But it doesn't have to be like this. There are simple methods of leaving uncomfortable situations much earlier – this way it's change *by choice* and not *by force*.

This book offers suggestions and exercises to become familiar with such methods.

We will encounter the term 'Conscious Breathing' in different chapters. It's a basic tool to move energies, emotions, feelings and also thoughts.

The concept of the 'Safe Space' will also appear in several sections. The Safe Space makes it easier for us to move from the old to the new and provides us with a feeling of security during the transition period.

....

The methods and exercises described in this book do not lay any claim to be a therapeutic approach.

They are intended solely for integration into daily life, to make it easier and more joyful.

12

Chapter 1

Conscious Breathing

Conscious BREATHING
Conscious LIVING
Conscious BEING

Breathing means living. Breathing means saying *Yes* to life. We start our life with the first breath and end it with the last one. In between, we consistently unlearn or simply forget how to breathe in a supportive way. We breathe unconsciously and shallowly, thus denying our body sufficient fresh energy.

This happens even though the importance of the breath has been known for millennia and various yoga techniques use it to influence and harmonize the energy flow within the human body. These techniques are applied less in Western countries and are now losing their relevance in the New Energy frequency of our growing consciousness, in which we are handling and manifesting things more easily and quickly.

Today it suffices to consciously let the breath flow, to consciously let it move in and out, with the emphasis here on *consciously*.

The more aware we are of our breath, the less we will get stuck in unwanted situations, the less we will dwell on angry and irritating everyday experiences or even fall ill.

Illnesses manifest when energies get stuck, when they are blocked. This often happens after traumatic experiences or when we work against our own best interests over a period of time – consciously or unconsciously. That's when we start compromising and stop living *our own* lives.

Regular conscious breathing allows blocked energies to flow again. Illnesses will manifest less frequently and those that have already manifested can now disappear.

We all know expressions like:

- I lost my breath
- It takes my breath away
- To gasp for breath
- To pant for air
- I first had to take a deep breath
- To be short of breath/to lose one's wind
- To hold one's breath
- To be out of breath
- To recover one's breath
- To regain one's breath

All these idioms express how important the breath is. We often hold our breath in stressful situations that take our breath away and then we gasp for breath or pant for air to regain our balance.

When we regularly practice conscious breathing, we will immediately remember it under such circumstances and be able to easily move out of stressful and traumatic situations. Conscious breathing allows us to quickly transform experiences that activate irritation and anger in us, so that we no longer carry this anger within us for days, weeks or even years.

Breathing Exercise

You can record this exercise on a CD and then listen to it with your loud speakers or headphones wherever you are.

- Take a deep breath.

- Feel the air flowing in. It gently caresses the inside of your nose.

- Breathe slowly in and out, in and out, in and out again.

- Feel how the energy expands within your body.

- You feel your body relaxing.

- Your face is completely relaxed. Your shoulders melt. Your chest is relaxed and opens up energetically. Your belly expands naturally. It relaxes and feels very comfortable.

- Take another deep breath.

- Feel the energy flowing through your legs, down to your feet and into the earth.

- You feel well grounded.

- Let go of all the problems that might be there and just be with your breath.

- Thoughts are coming, thoughts are going, the breath remains – it flows in and out.

- Breathe gently in your own rhythm. Breathe in and breathe out, in and out again.

- To eventually come back into the Now, take a few deep conscious breaths.

- Be aware of your body, the floor beneath your feet, the chair you are sitting or the couch you are lying on. You can stretch your body and move your toes and fingers.

- Feel your entire body and breathe consciously, deep conscious breaths, until you feel very present.

Practice this exercise, whenever you want to take some time for *yourself.*

Mastering Stressful Situations
by Conscious Breathing

It has probably already happened to all of us that someone in the street, in a shop or in the office vents his rage at us, insults us or just treats us unkindly.

When this happens, take a deep breath and be very aware of your breath. By keeping your attention on your own breath, you will notice that you don't get caught in the other's bad mood. You will not feel hurt and you won't get angry, because the anger that might arise will begin to fade away. It can be so easy, as long as we remember to take that first deep breath.

The more often you practice this conscious breathing, the more quickly you will think of it when you find yourself in such a situation.

Gradually you will develop a kind of automatic response, which you will often only notice after you've taken that first deep breath. With a new sense of ease and with calm detachment you can now observe what you have just experienced.

Resolving Guilt Feelings by Conscious Breathing

We all know them, these nagging, annoying feelings … feelings of guilt.

They show up when we have taken on responsibility for something or someone and we are now unable or just unwilling to carry that responsibility any longer and we don't know how to end this situation.

The word *responsibility* contains the word *response*. When we take responsibility for something, we respond to what we have initiated, caused or done. *We* give - so to speak - the appropriate answers.

But as soon as we take responsibility for someone else, we answer for something that this person has initiated, caused, done or is about to do. *We* answer in his place. Metaphorically speaking, we cut him off, often believing that we know better than he what is best for him.

Our ego takes over. We behave arrogantly, applying our standards instead of honoring those of this other person.

When the responsibility then gets too big for us and we cannot or don't want to carry it any longer, feelings of guilt arise. Here too, conscious breathing can be very helpful.

Breathing Exercise

- Sit quietly on your chair and take a deep breath.

- When did you take responsibility for someone, which you cannot and/or don't want to carry any longer? This is probably the reason for your guilt feeling.

- Go consciously into the feeling. How do you experience this guilt feeling? Is there a gnawing in the stomach area? Is there a sudden headache, a rumbling in your belly or does some other part of your body hurt?

- Also be aware of the feeling behind all this, the feeling that you probably want to get rid of, because it makes you feel rather uncomfortable.

- Now take a deep breath. Allow your breath to flow into your body and be very aware of this natural flow. Focus on your conscious and calm breath.

- Accept this uncomfortable feeling, let go of any resistance to it, accept it and ... *breathe.*

- Breathe and observe if the feeling is changing, how it is changing.

- Everything is perfect the way it is.

- Imagine now what it is like to hand the responsibility back to the one who is truly responsible for these 'responses' that you have been supplying up to now.

- Breathe – how does it feel to hand back the responsibility?

- Is there a feeling of ease, is there a sudden feeling of worthlessness or emptiness, or does it just feel different?

- Whatever feeling arises, allow it in, do *not* analyze it, *nor* try to define it. Just *breathe*.

- *Breathe - allow - let go - breathe - allow - let go* - find *your own* rhythm.

- End this exercise with a deep, conscious breath.

Perhaps answers to the current situation have already arrived during the exercise.

I have often observed while breathing consciously that 'answers' simply arrive, without even having asked any questions.

All solutions are already there.

Summary ...

Breathing consciously moves energies that are about to get stuck as well as energies we have been blocking for a long time for various reasons. Energies want to move. They want to flow. But often we only allow them to flow after having been badly struck by fate or when we are in difficult situations and there is nothing else left to do, but to let go of everything.

It does not have to be like this. Integrating conscious breathing into our everyday life enables us to handle potential challenges much more easily and much more gracefully.

You will also encounter conscious breathing in the following chapters of this book because it is the most natural and easiest way to move energies. It brings a graceful flow into our life and maintains it.

Chapter 2

The Safe Space

Those who give up freedom
in order to gain security
will end up losing both
Benjamin Franklin

We tend to strive constantly for security. We purchase insurance policies, look for a permanent, *secure* job or a partner with a *secure* income, we *secure* partners with marriage contracts and vows and we *secure* agreements with contracts.

Looking for external security is very common and most people consider it normal or even extremely important. But does this external security really help if we feel insecure inside?

External security covers at best the financial aspect. But only the one, who discovers a feeling of security *within*, will *be* truly secure.

What helps us here is the concept of the *Safe Space*. This safe space is not to be understood literally. It is not spatially limited, nor is it an energy shield you build around yourself. It is simply a feeling, an inner security.

But how do I get to this safe space? How can I create it?

The first step is: *I choose it*. I make a conscious choice to be in a safe space. The second step is I take a deep, conscious breath to fill this space, this inner security with strength and energy.

Too simple? Try it out and then feel into you. Has anything changed? Do you feel safer, lighter, different? You can repeat these two steps at any time and apply them in everyday life, whenever you feel like it.

Here too, practice makes perfect! In my experience, the feeling of security intensifies, the more I consciously choose my safe space.

Only when we feel safe and secure within, can true independence, sovereignty and freedom gracefully unfold.

When does the Safe Space help?

- When feelings of fear come up, like the fear of exams, or of failure, but also fears you cannot really put your finger on

- in stressful situations

- when you feel lonely

- before falling asleep

- when you are suffering from sleep disorders

- when thoughts keep spinning around in your head

- when you feel under pressure

- when you are in doubt

- whenever you feel insecure

then

- take a deep breath

- choose your safe space

- take another deep breath and

- continue breathing - slowly and consciously, in your own rhythm

At night, before falling asleep, I often consciously create my safe space. It makes me feel relaxed and secure.

Chapter 3

The Observer

Observing rather than getting involved
Perceiving reality in self awareness

So often we become entangled in discussions, justifications, arguments, feelings of guilt and so many other unwanted things.

Afterwards, we ask ourselves how the whole thing developed as it did. Or we get caught up in a train of arguments that we 'definitely will bring up next time'. But from whatever perspective we look at it, the situation remains unsatisfactory, and we don't feel good about it at all.

How can we change this?

One possibility in such cases is that we become the observer. To become an observer means to decide consciously to step out of a situation, a conversation or an argument and switch to the observer role instead of remaining the protagonist.

However, this can be quite difficult in many situations, as we have often already internalized this specific mode of 'personal interaction', especially in our families, in relationships, but also in our jobs.

Again and again we become entangled in the same processes, conversations and actions, often over many years and, to an extent, always respond in the same way. We go around in circles and take our own feelings and those of the others on a roller coaster ride.

Only as the observer can we finally detect the intentions of the other and our role in this game. We can now clearly see things as they really are. We are no longer trapped in the old game, but have the possibility to respond differently. Patterns that don't serve us any longer can be transformed.

This observer role not only helps us in our daily life. It can also support us when dealing with world events that descend on us every day in headlines and reports and follow us right into our living rooms via television, radio and the internet.

Again we can slip into the observer role here, once we realize that we lose our balance by getting involved in what we see, hear or read. From this detached position we are able to perceive the real context, without becoming judgmental due to our own emotions.

We are now able to detect manipulations, so that they will quickly lose their effect on us. We realize that every experience and each message contains many facets, depending on how we look at them.

So how do we become an observer?

Whenever you notice that you are being drawn into what's happening around you, consciously take a deep breath and make a clear decision to switch to the observer role.

Then sense your feelings. There could be feelings of anger, sadness, shame, self-doubt, frustration, rage or some kind of joy. Yes, even joy can consciously be created by others to entice you. Praise, for example, is not always heartfelt, it is also used for manipulative purposes.

You'll notice the difference as soon as you consciously observe your feelings and the accompanying physical reactions. Breathe and continue to observe, now from this new position.

Initially it might not be so easy for you to remember that you can step out of these situations at any time, but again, the more often you practice it, the more quickly you will be aware of this possibility.

So, as soon as you realize that you are becoming entangled in a situation, or you see such a situation beginning to develop:

- Take a deep breath.
- Choose consciously to go into the observer role.

- Observe both the others and yourself, and
- then act from this detached position.
- Observe how your reactions are changing ... and *breathe*.

Chapter 4

The Answers within

They exist, the answers within.
Listen to them – Feel them –
Experience them – Live them.

Usually we seek answers to our questions outside of ourselves. We ask friends for advice and doctors to heal us. We read magazines, to find out how to dress or what to eat.

Most of the time we direct our attention outwards. We rarely take the time to really journey inwards, pretending to *have* no time. I've always liked the saying: "You don't *have* time. You *take* time."

We all have 24 hours available per day. How we spend those 24 hours, how we use them, spread them over our various activities is up to each one of us.

Some people have good time management skills, others plan in such a way that they have the feeling of never having enough time, or even of being under time pressure.

There is a variety of reasons for this:

- perhaps we can never say *no* when others ask us for something - whether it's a family member, colleagues, clients or the boss or

- we are constantly running away from ourselves, we do not feel comfortable with ourselves and therefore make far too many appointments with far too many people or

- we want to make a fast buck and use all our time doing this, including the time we then lack for leisure activities.

You will have *your* own reasons, if you never *have* time.

However, in order to find *yourself* and the answers *within*, it is essential that you take time for yourself, that you listen to yourself and that you regularly tune into yourself.

This does not mean spending time analyzing or exploring the causes for something. It means just being with yourself.

The inner voice responds best in silence, when you concentrate only on yourself and your breath. It's perfectly okay when thoughts pop up. Just let them come. They will go after a while when you let them be.

When you realize that your mind is starting to wander ...

- ... take a conscious breath.

- Concentrate on your breath as it flows smoothly in and out.

- You don't have to do anything. It flows by itself.

- Just observe.

- You gradually feel your body relaxing and the weight falling from your shoulders.

- You've broken through this constant train of thoughts.

- Once you feel calm and you are totally aware of yourself, ask yourself your question.

- Breathe in and let it go.

- Perhaps there is an immediate answer, or maybe you only feel emptiness.

- Do *not* start to ponder on your question or your feelings. Let them go and concentrate only on your breath.

- You complete the exercise with a deep, conscious breath.

The answers will come - maybe immediately, maybe the next day or the next week.

You can be sure that sooner or later each of your questions will be answered. Maybe the topic comes your way from the outside or you have a sudden idea or get an impulse.

The Writing Method

If you enjoy writing, you can also find *your* answers in the following way. Before falling asleep, when you're lying relaxed in bed, ask yourself a question that is important for you at the moment. Do not think about it afterwards, just let it go and breathe consciously.

The next morning take a piece of paper and write down whatever comes up. Your topic will be there, too. As you allow the words to flow onto the paper without any interruption, a response to your question can take shape. Often you will suddenly find a new way of looking at things or your perspective on an old view shifts and expands.

While writing, 'switch your mind off' as much as possible and do not *think* about what you want to write next. Thinking stops the flow and the answers *within* will be distorted by the mind.

So, don't stop writing, just write down whatever pops into your mind. Surprise yourself!

36

Chapter 5

House-Cleaning

As the Outside, so the Inside
As in Macro, so in Micro
As the House, so the Resident

As the Outside, so the Inside

Who does not know the pleasant feeling of sitting happily and contented in a neat and tidy home, after having cleaned the house or apartment?

But a thorough house-cleaning is so much more. The numerous unnecessary and outworn things that we accumulate around us over time should also be continually adapted to our current situation, and, if necessary, be removed.

Not only do unused things occupy space, they also prevent energy from flowing. Wherever things remain stationary for a period of time, energy blockages will develop, and the well-known saying, 'As the Outside, so the Inside' applies here, too.

The blocked energy around us - in cupboards, drawers, shelves – also manifests within us. It impedes us in our life. We get stuck and have problems making decisions.

Therefore a thorough 'outer house-cleaning' also includes removing unused things - whether we throw out the various items, give them to someone or sell them.

In addition to this 'outer house-cleaning' there is also an 'inner house-cleaning' when we change direction in areas of our life that no longer feel good.

We generally have known for quite a while that we need to take another step in life, or that something entirely new is required to bring joy back into our life. But still we have not yet decided to make that change. This could be at work, in our relationship or in our living arrangements.

The 'Outer House-Cleaning'

Often it is easier to start with the outer house-cleaning, i.e. in our own house or apartment. So, let's get started!

First of all take a look around your room - very consciously and calmly. You will discover a lot of things that you haven't used for a long time or that you don't even notice anymore - even things that are easily visible in the room.

You may notice that you have read many of your books just once and since then just dusted them once in a while, or you discover a lot of clothes in your closet that you have not worn in years.

Holiday souvenirs you don't even notice anymore - except when dusting them. Yet they stand on chests of drawers and shelves, and for the umpteenth time you see the unwanted gift that bothers you every time you have it in your hands or when it catches your eye.

Now it is time to let them go. Maybe it helps that you have just realized that it's these things that are blocking you, that rob your energy every time they bother you.

After having cleared the living area, you can now go to the basement. There are often things stored here that have been long forgotten. If you need them, you'll probably buy new ones, because you don't even know they are still there.

Or, packed boxes from your last move are still lying in the basement years later. You could actually dispose of them without even opening them. You really haven't missed the contents in all this time. But we usually haven't got the heart to do that.

So, if you can't do it, look through everything again and then, being aware that superfluous things block you, dispose of them, give them away, or sell them.

Tips on how to separate more easily

Of course we all are different. There are people who separate more easily from the Old and people who have the greatest problems with it.

But be aware that when you are unable to separate from things that don't serve you anymore, you are emotionally attached to the Old. There is then no room for the New that best suits your current situation and fits you better *now*. When you hold on to the Old, you get stuck in it and this deprives you of new experiences.

A trick I use now: I take pictures of the things I'm still emotionally attached to. I then find it easier to give them away. I discovered doing this that it's not really important for me that I still can touch these things. The memories and feelings that I associate with them are also there when I just look at the picture. Sooner or later, the picture, too, loses its importance. The emotional connection has been severed.

What makes us still want to keep things? We have convinced ourselves that we might soon need what we intend to give away, even if we have not used it for years.

Changing my approach has helped me here. I tell myself now: "if I need one item from the twenty things I gave away, I'll buy it again and am glad that the other 19 are no longer blocking my energy." And isn't it nice, to have a newer version of something after a while?

As soon as the outer house-cleaning is finished ... you've separated from old books, from clothes you don't wear anymore, from unwanted gifts, and in the basement you only have things you are still using ... you can start the 'inner house-cleaning'.

However, you probably already realize that your home and your life feel lighter and more spacious. Even if it's not really visible that the apartment is emptier, cupboards filled with fewer items do feel different from overloaded ones. The energy is flowing again, and you can feel it.

The 'Inner House-Cleaning'

When cleaning your 'inner house', it is important to understand in which areas of your life you are compromising.

Perhaps you would have liked to change apartment for quite a while - get an apartment in another neighborhood, another city, larger or smaller - but you never actually started looking for it.

Or you don't feel any joy in your job anymore. You would rather be self-employed, work in another line of business or your boss is giving you a hard time.

Or you're in a relationship, which has become more a burden than a joy.

Whatever aspect of your life is not as you would *actually* like it to be, look at it, feel deeply into it and breathe! If you really want to change something - now is the time to let go of these compromises step by step.

Compromises

We speak of foul compromises. Are there really other kinds?

When we - for whatever reason - compromise, we lie to ourselves, we deceive ourselves and all the others who are involved in this compromise. We are not being honest with ourselves. We invent excuses for ourselves and for others.

When we practice this for some time, we no longer know at some point what we *really* want and what is *really* important for us. We gradually lose clarity.

We come to terms with unwanted situations. Eventually we can no longer imagine that we could instead live a comfortable, easy life, one in tune with our dreams.

So why are we compromising?

Depending on our personality and our individual history, there are many different reasons for this, yet almost everybody knows them in some form.

We often compromise for example for the sake of peace and quiet.

We keep quiet when we actually should say something to make our position clear to others. We do not want to *confront* ourselves.

The word 'con*front*' contains parts of the word *frontier*. In order to confront ourselves, we would have to go to frontiers, maybe even go beyond and raise our voices. For the sake of peace, however, we prefer to compromise and, in doing so, limit ourselves.

We also make compromises in order to preserve harmony. The question now arises: "Is there still harmony, when it becomes necessary to preserve it?" Looking at the situation from the outside, it may seem as if it would have remained balanced, but the imbalance is now inside the one who has compromised.

We compromise in order to avoid being alone. The harder it is for us to feel good just being with ourselves, the more we are willing to compromise in our relationships.

Compromises are made so as to be seen by others as a 'nice guy', to be loved, to maintain a relationship, to keep the family together, to feel financially safe, to have more money, to not have to make a change, to not have to be creative, to not have to overcome our own laziness or to not have to take responsibility.

These are all compromises with which we restrict, limit and hinder ourselves and ultimately keep true joy out of our lives.

But how do we stop 'compromising'?

The first step is always to become aware of it. To recognize that we live lives of compromise and to honestly admit it can be painful at first. We certainly need plenty of deep breaths here to get the energy flowing again, an energy that may have been stuck for a long time.

Allow yourself the time to gain this awareness, whether it is during a walk in a forest or sitting on your couch at home. Take your time to clearly recognize your compromises. Don't try to define them, analyze them or to find reasons why they are there. That only raises new questions. Just look at them and *breathe*.

Breathing Session

- Take a deep breath.

- Choose your safe space.

- Sense how your compromise feels, the compromise that you've just discovered, or that you perhaps have only really admitted for the first time. Maybe it feels uncomfortable.

- Continue your calm breathing and allow this feeling.

- Just let it *be* and move with the breath.

- Stay with your breath for a while. Inhale gently and exhale, inhale and exhale

- and feel.

Maybe that's already enough for the first day or for the first few days.

Feel how quickly you want to and/or are able to go ahead.

When you are ready … go to the next step, which is to ask yourself: "What do I *really* want to have in this area of my life"?

Leave aside all internal objections that may arise while asking this question. It's all about coming back to *your* clarity.

What do you really want?

Once you are clear, that which you have regarded as obstacles until now can quickly dissolve.

Breathing Session

- Sit comfortably on a chair - your feet are on the ground.

- Close your eyes.

- Take a deep breath.

- What do you feel when you think about the area of your life you want to change?

- How does it feel *right now*?

- Allow your feelings. They are all fine.

- Breathe consciously for a while, in and out, in and out again.

- Then ask yourself: What do I *really* want? How do I *really* want to live this part of my life?

- It's fine if there are inner images. Look at them and stay with your feelings.

- Breathe consciously ... one breath at a time.

- Perhaps some kind of fear comes up when you feel into your *new* situation, or perhaps pure joy. Whatever.

- It doesn't matter what's coming up, but rather how you deal with it.

- Breathe and feel. Feel into the new situation.

- Breathe for several minutes and observe your feelings.

- Finish the exercise with a deep, conscious breath.

You can repeat this exercise at any time.

Once clarity is achieved, the next step is the *conscious choice*.

Chapter 6

Conscious Choice

Choose joyfully.
Choose clearly.
Choose regularly.
And your life will change!!!

To a large extent we have unlearned how to be the creators of our own lives.

Every day we allow our employers to tell us what we have to do - for them. Food, fashion, manners and even leisure activities with their various kinds of in-sports and trends are dictated to us from the outside and ... we let them be dictated to us.

Often others pretend to know better than we do what is good for us. We believe them and adjust our lives accordingly.

Sooner or later we feel dependent, oppressed that fate has dealt us a blow and a false certainty grows in us that we are at the mercy of all this.

We have lost the inner knowingness that we *always* have the choice to shape and to change our lives.

We often hear ourselves say:

- I had no choice.
- Do I really have a choice?
- I had no other choice, but …
- If I could do as I want, I would …
- I cannot decide it myself.
- I first have to come to an agreement.

All this shows that we are convinced we have no choice, that we cannot make our own decisions and that we are not able or allowed to choose until we have first gone through the process of consultations, through agreements or compromises.

And yet the conscious choice is the most powerful and simplest tool we have to really direct our own lives. By choosing consciously, our hopes and dreams no longer remain stuck in a desire or dream stage, they really do come true.

Once we make our choice, take a clear decision, all the energies around us start to align. Our choice begins to manifest.

Actually we have all experienced this already. We decide on something and suddenly this very subject appears all around us.

We tell someone about it, and this person has the necessary contacts for us or maybe has just read an article on the topic and can help us with this knowledge.

We get all the help we need from the universe. But we are the only ones who can then commit to it and take the next steps.

If our choice doesn't manifest, it might be that the difference between wishing and choosing is unclear to us, i.e. we believe that if we wish for something, we automatically choose it. It is not like that!

Wishing is something airy and vague, that may or may not be real. We long for something, we hope for something, but we do not really want to take responsibility for it. It would be nice, if ...

The *choice*, however, is a clear decision for or against something. We decide what we really want. There is a completely different energy in a choice; it's the power of personal responsibility. *We* are committed to it. *We* made our choice.

If it still does not manifest, then either there is a lack of patience or old and often unconscious beliefs are blocking our plans.

After each decision, it is therefore helpful to feel into it:

- How does it feel to have made this decision?
- Do I fully stand behind it?
- Am I really *happy* with this decision?
- Do I feel relieved?

or

- Are there doubts coming up?
- Is there a scary feeling coming up?
- Do I somehow feel uncomfortable with it?

These feelings of rejection are often triggered unconsciously, for example, if we have experienced failure in similar situations in the past, as well as by old convictions, beliefs or religious influences.

Whatever may be the trigger: *The universe responds directly.*

If our fears and doubts are in the foreground, then the universe helps to manifest them. We can therefore assume that it's truly we who are blocking the manifestation of our decisions ... unconsciously of course.

So, what can we do?

Here too, the solution is the conscious breath. When you notice that you feel uncomfortable after having made a decision, when worries, fears and/or doubts are coming up, then:

- Take a deep breath.

- Choose your safe space.

- Sense where you perceive this feeling.

- Send your next breath to this place and continue breathing, calmly and regularly.

- Breathe in - breathe out and

- continue observing yourself, without judging, without wanting to work out the source of your fears or doubts.

- Just breathe - for several minutes - and

- observe yourself.

Perhaps the uncomfortable feelings disappear, perhaps they don't. Perhaps you're just not *yet* ready for *this* decision. If you are not comfortable with your decision, even after the breathing exercise *choose something else*. You always have the option to do this. Give *yourself* permission!!! *Choose*!!!

Perhaps it's sufficient to just vary your previous choice slightly in order to really feel good about it. Perhaps, being really honest with yourself, you want to choose something completely different. If this is the case, make a different choice. Choose, and let things unfold.

Whenever you don't choose for yourself, you give someone else the power to be your master. Only by choosing consciously, will *you* become the master of *your* life.

Chapter 7

The Breathing Sessions at a Glance

1. You can apply this breathing session any time you want to take a few minutes for *yourself.*

   - Take a deep breath.

   - Feel the air flowing in; it gently caresses the inside of your nose.

   - Breathe slowly in and out, in and out, in and out again.

   - Feel how the energy expands within your body.

   - You feel your body relaxing.

   - Your face is completely relaxed. Your shoulders melt. Your chest is relaxed and opens up energetically. Your belly expands naturally. It relaxes and feels very comfortable.

   - Take another deep breath.

   - Feel the energy flowing through your legs, down to your feet and into the earth.

- You feel well grounded.

- Let go of all the problems that might be there and just be with your breath.

- Thoughts are coming, thoughts are going, the breath remains – it flows in and out.

- Breathe gently in your own rhythm. Breathe in and breathe out, in and out again.

- To eventually come back into the Now, take a few deep conscious breaths.

- Be aware of your body, the floor beneath your feet, the chair you are sitting or the couch you are lying on. You can stretch your body and move your toes and fingers.

- Feel your entire body and breathe consciously, deep conscious breaths, until you feel very present.

2. Clearing Guilt Feelings

Breathing Session

- Sit quietly on your chair and take a deep breath.

- When did you take responsibility for someone, which you cannot and/or don't want to carry any longer? This is probably the reason for your guilt feeling.

- Go consciously into the feeling. How do you experience this guilt feeling? Is there a gnawing in the stomach area? Is there a sudden headache, a rumbling in your belly or does some other part of your body hurt?

- Also be aware of the feeling behind all this, the feeling that you probably want to get rid of, because it makes you feel rather uncomfortable.

- Now take a deep breath. Allow your breath to flow into your body and be very aware of this natural flow. Focus on your conscious and calm breath.

- Accept this uncomfortable feeling, let go of any resistance to it, accept it and ... *breathe*.

- Breathe and observe if the feeling is changing, how it is changing.

- Everything is perfect the way it is.

- Imagine now what it is like to hand the responsibility back to the one who is truly responsible for these 'responses' that you have been supplying up to now.

- Breathe – how does it feel to hand back the responsibility?

- Is there a feeling of ease, is there a sudden feeling of worthlessness or emptiness, or does it just feel different?

- Whatever feeling arises, allow it in, do *not* analyze it, *nor* try to define it. Just *breathe*.

- *Breathe - allow - let go - breathe - allow - let go* - find *your own* rhythm.

    - End this exercise with a deep, conscious breath.

3. Finding *Your* Answers

Breathing Session

- Take a conscious breath.

- Concentrate on your breath as it flows smoothly in and out.

- You don't have to do anything. It flows by itself.

- Just observe.

- You gradually feel your body relaxing and the weight falling from your shoulders.

- You've broken through this constant train of thoughts.

- Once you feel calm and you are totally aware of yourself, ask yourself your question.

- Breathe in and let it go.

- Perhaps there is an immediate answer, or maybe you only feel emptiness.

- Do *not* start to ponder on your question or your feelings. Let them go and concentrate only on your breath.

- You complete the exercise with a deep, conscious breath.

The answers will come - maybe immediately, maybe the next day or the next week.

You can be sure that sooner or later each of your questions will be answered. Maybe the topic comes your way from the outside or you have a sudden idea or get an impulse.

4. Identifying and Clearing Compromises

Breathing Session

- Take a deep breath.

- Choose your safe space.

- Sense how your compromise feels, the compromise that you've just discovered, or that you perhaps have only really admitted for the first time. Maybe it feels uncomfortable.

- Continue your calm breathing and allow this feeling.

- Just let it *be* and move with the breath.

- Stay with your breath for a while. Inhale gently and exhale, inhale and exhale

- and feel.

- When you are ready ask yourself: "What do I *really* want? How do I *really* want to live this part of my life"?

- Take a deep breath.

- What do you feel now when you think about the area of your life you want to change?

- How does it feel *right now*?

- Allow your feelings. They are all fine.

- Breathe consciously for a while, in and out, in and out again.

- It's fine if there are inner images. Look at them and stay with your feelings.

- Breathe consciously ... one breath at a time.

- Perhaps some kind of fear comes up when you feel into your *new* situation, or perhaps pure joy. Whatever.

- It doesn't matter what's coming up, but rather how you deal with it.

- Breathe and feel. Feel into the new situation.

- Breathe for several minutes and observe your feelings.

- Finish the exercise with a deep, conscious breath.

Epilog

Living more Consciously - Step by Step

It is advisable to work *regularly* with the exercises and suggestions given in the previous chapters. A certain automatic response can only develop when you practice regularly and consciously.

If someone then treats you disrespectfully, shouts at you or attempts to control you, you will automatically take a conscious breath, create your safe space and make a clear choice to switch to the observer role.

All this will make your life easier. You now react more calmly, your feelings do not overwhelm you anymore, and the reactions of others may also be calmer than they would have otherwise been. If not, it will no longer rattle you.

By practicing the exercises described above regularly and by breathing consciously, our blockages and old beliefs, formed over many years and many lifetimes, can also dissolve gradually, layer by layer.

Your reactions are changing, and you'll be surprised at how differently you approach and overcome problems and how quickly you'll find solutions. There will no longer be this mental chattering for days and weeks, revolving around the same subject.

Taking time *for you* at least once a week to listen to the answers within, will improve your intuition, and the answers will come to you more and more quickly. Remember: you and you alone are the time manager of your life!

A thorough house-cleaning also takes time, time which only you can provide. It can even be fun in the end to create more living and breathing space. Try it out!

The 'ultimate' tool is the *conscious choice*. When choosing always remember: the more thoroughly you did your inner and outer house-cleaning, the fewer compromises you are now making in your life, the more clearly you know what you really want and what gives you joy, the more quickly and easily your choices manifest and come into your reality.

Magic is possible.
Create YOUR own world!!!

Thanks

A *huge thank you* to Carmel Finnan for her professional proofreading.

Many thanks to Veronika Peschkes for her graphic support.

Thanks to all my dear friends and acquaintances, who listened to my private readings and encouraged me to publish what they heard.

And finally, *thanks* to myself for daring to start this book project and bringing it into being ☺.